Let's Make More Money

An *Exclusive* Guide for
Kurti Retailers on Wealth Creation

Let's Make More Money

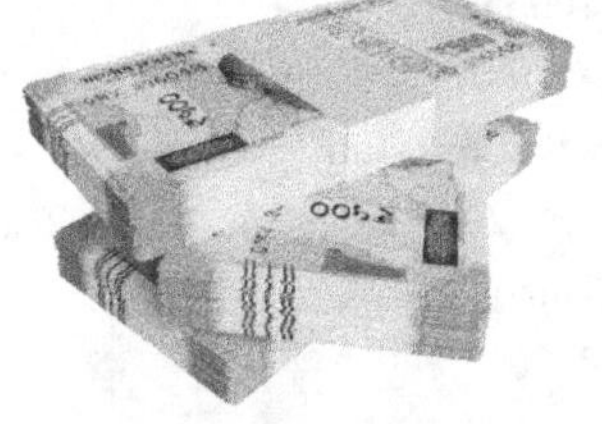

An *Exclusive* Guide for
Kurti Retailers on Wealth Creation

VIKAS N BANURA

Worldwide Published by
Pendown Press

PENDOWN PRESS LLP
An ISO 9001 & ISO 14001 Certified Co.
Regd. Office 3767A, Kanhaiya Nagar,
Tri Nagar, Delhi-110035
Ph.: 8180886000, 9650072927, 8595249536
E-mail: info@pendownpress.com
Branch Office 1A/2A, 20, Hari Sadan, Ansari Road,
Daryaganj, New Delhi-110002
Ph.: 011-45794768
Website: PendownPress.com

First Edition: 2023

ISBN: 978-93-5554-623-4

Layout and Cover Designed by Pendown Graphics Team
Printed and Bound in India by Thomson Press India Ltd.

Thank You

To my father, your teachings have shaped my foundation, guiding me towards success.

To the inspiring retailers, your drive and passion motivate me to reach new heights.

To my mentor, Akshar Yadav, your guidance and support have been invaluable on this journey.

I am grateful for the lessons, inspiration, and unwavering belief in my potential.

This book is a tribute to the impact each of you has had on my life and success.

With heartfelt appreciation,

~Vikas N Banura

Contents

Preface

Welcome to the exciting world of "Let's Make More Money". I am thrilled to introduce this comprehensive guide, which will assist you in unlocking the secrets to achieving financial success in your business.

Finance can often feel overwhelming and complicated, but I firmly believe that it doesn't have to be. Through this book, my objective is to simplify finance and present it in a manner that is accessible and easy to understand for all readers.

Drawing upon my own experiences as an entrepreneur and fueled by my passion for finance, I have carefully distilled powerful strategies that can propel your business towards greater heights. From budgeting and cash flow management to growth strategies and cost control measures, these strategies are designed to make a tangible difference in your business's financial health.

Throughout the pages, you will discover practical advice, real-life examples, and step-by-step guidance to help you implement these strategies effectively. I have written this book with the intention of empowering you to make well-informed financial decisions and build a solid foundation for long-term success.

Foreword

In this book, Vikas delves deep into the essential strategies that have the power to revolutionize your business and create a path towards financial success. The insights and practical advice shared within these pages are truly invaluable, offering a roadmap to navigate the complexities of finance and make well-informed decisions.

What sets this book apart is Vikas's genuine passion for empowering retailers and business owners. His commitment to simplifying complex financial concepts and making them accessible to all readers is commendable. The strategies presented here are actionable and have the potential to revolutionize your financial management practices.

I have personally witnessed Vikas's dedication and expertise in the field, and his ability to translate that knowledge into practical guidance is truly remarkable. I have no doubt that the strategies outlined in this book will provide you with the tools to take your business to new heights.

Whether you are an experienced business owner or just starting on your entrepreneurial journey, "Let's Make More Money" is a must-read. It offers a wealth of insights and strategies that can transform your financial mindset and position your business for long-term growth and prosperity.

I applaud Vikas for his passion, expertise, and commitment to helping others achieve financial success. It is with great pleasure that I endorse this book and recommend it to anyone seeking to unlock the potential of their business through sound financial strategies.

~Naveen N Banura

Women's Fashion Retail Expert

Introduction

Welcome to the world of **"Let's Make More Money."** In this book, we will explore practical strategies that can help you thrive in the business world. Whether you run a retail business or own a company, this book is designed to provide you with the tools and knowledge you need to achieve financial success.

Throughout the chapters, we will cover important topics such as budgeting, managing your money flow, and planning for the future. We will also discuss strategies for growing your business and controlling costs,. Real-life examples and step-by-step advice will be shared to assist you in applying these strategies to your own business.

My aim is to make finance easy to understand, even if you don't have much prior knowledge. I want to empower you to make smart decisions, maximize your resources, and set yourself up for long-term growth. With a solid financial foundation and the right strategies, you can overcome challenges and achieve your goals.

I encourage you to approach this book with an open mind and a willingness to learn. Each chapter builds upon the previous one, creating a roadmap for your financial success.

Take a moment to reflect on your own business practices, identify areas for improvement, and embrace new ideas that can assist you in moving forward.

Thank you for joining me on this journey. I am excited to share these valuable insights with you and witness how they can positively impact your business and personal growth. Let's embark on the path to financial success together. *Chalo Paisa Banate hai!*

My Story

Hello, friends! My name is Vikas Banura, and I have always been passionate about finance. I began my career working as an executive at ICICI Bank, but deep inside, I always nurtured a dream of becoming an entrepreneur. So, I made the bold decision to take a leap and relocated to Jaipur with my elder brother to start our own business selling women's ethnic sarees.

In the beginning, things went well, and soon our business became successful. However, after four to five years, we encountered a significant problem. Our business started to fail because we had not properly planned our finances. We accumulated a substantial amount of debt and lacked a reliable source of income. This situation had a negative impact on our entire family, causing us all to became deeply concerned.

During this difficult time, we identified an opportunity in the market. Ready-made dresses for women, especially ethnic wear, were not very popular. After conducting a thorough market analysis, we realized that there was a big demand for ready-made kurtis. We thought of creating stylish and affordable clothing options for women. Drawing upon my 15 years of experience in the industry and with the support of my brother, we started a new venture.

Even though starting our new business wasn't easy, and we faced many challenges along the way, our passion for finance and our market understanding kept us motivated. We exerted considerable effort to carefully plan our finances wisely and make intelligent decisions. Gradually, we started to turn things around. People loved the quality and affordability of our products, and our brand gained popularity.

As years went by, our business continued to progress. We expanded our range of products by offering more variety and gained a loyal customer base. Our commitment to effective financial management helped us to overcome the earlier difficulties and thrive in a highly competitive industry.

Today, our company stands as an example illustrating the importance of being resilient and understanding finance. We have not only achieved financial stability but also created employment opportunities for others. Our journey taught us the value of planning our finances carefully, adapting to changes in the market, and seizing opportunities when they come our way.

Looking back, I am grateful for the failures and challenges we endured. They taught us valuable lessons and shaped us into successful entrepreneurs we are today. I still have a strong passion for finance, and I want to help others navigate the business world using my knowledge and the lessons I've learned.

Always remember, setbacks do not signify the end of the road; instead, they present opportunities for growth and improvement. With the right understanding of finance and a determined spirit, you can conquer any obstacle and make your dreams come true.

Chapter 1

Introduction to Finance

Finance, in simple terms, refers to the funds necessary to operate a business. Basically, it is managing all the incoming and outgoing funds. It is not only the money required for commercial and personal purposes but also the funds that business owners need to sustain and expand the businesses while fulfilling their family and personal needs.

Finance encompasses the management of money, investments, and resources within a business.

It involves making financial decisions, analyzing financial data, and allocating funds effectively.

Understanding finance is crucial for business owners to navigate the financial landscape.

Importance of Finance in Business Growth

Unlike salaried individuals, business owners do not have a fixed monthly income, and they withdraw money from the business as needed. Challenges arise when there is a shortage of funds during financial needs, as funds may be tied in stocks, debtors, or capital assets.

Business owners may appear to be earning money on paper, but in reality, they may be burdened with debt. They may have no actual balance in the bank and lack contingency plans.

The COVID-19 pandemic has demonstrated that unforeseen circumstances can significantly impact businesses. It highlights the importance of being prepared for such situations in the future. Finance is a very important part of any business, as we have witnessed large companies fail due to poor financial management. It is not only beneficial for business growth and stability but also for personal growth and development.

Effective financial management is crucial for sustainable business growth and stability.

Additionally, developing a financial mindset is crucial for business owners to effectively manage their finances, make informed decisions, and position themselves for long-term success. A financial mindset facilitates improved resource allocation, risk management, and the navigation of complex financial matters.

My aim is to provide business owners with a solid foundation in finance and the importance of effective financial management. By understanding the basics of finance, recognizing the significance of prioritizing profit extraction, and adopting a financial mindset, business owners are better equipped to make informed decisions and propel their enterprises toward long-term success and sustainability.

Chapter 2

Need and Desire: Unveiling the Difference

"If you buy things you do not need, Soon you will have to sell things you need."

~Warren Buffet

There comes an important difference between need and desire.

Needs are essential for the operation and survival of a business. They encompass basic infrastructure, necessary resources, and essential services. On the other hand, wants refer to desires that are not crucial for the core functioning of the business but have the potential to enhance its operations or aesthetics.

Here are a few examples to illustrate the point:

- A business owner may need a four-wheeler for transportation purposes, but his desire might be to own a BMW.

- A business may require a standard desktop or laptop computer for everyday operations, but the desire of individuals within the organization may be to have MAC/Apple devices.

- If you use business receipts to satisfy personal desires instead of prioritizing the needs of the business, it can have a detrimental effect on the working capital. This can ultimately lead to business failure.

- So, you should clearly differentiate between your needs and desires.

- Emphasizing the importance of identifying and fulfilling essential needs before allocating resources to wants is crucial.

- Whenever you find yourself in need of something, take a moment to assess whether it is a genuine need or simply a desire.

- If it is a need, go for it; if it is a desire, wait before spending money on it .

- For desires, you should develop a wealth plan.

- Spend money on desires when they transition into needs or when you have accumulated sufficient wealth for that desire. In the upcoming chapters, you will learn about creating a plan for wealth accumulation.

- By understanding the distinction between needs and wants and making informed decisions, business owners can prioritize essential needs while selectively incorporating wants to support growth and maintain financial stability.

- Use your money to acquire assets not liabilities.

Chapter 3

The Power of Planning

- SMART goals, which stands for (Specific, Measurable, Achievable, Relevant, Time-bound) are instrumental in creating actionable targets.

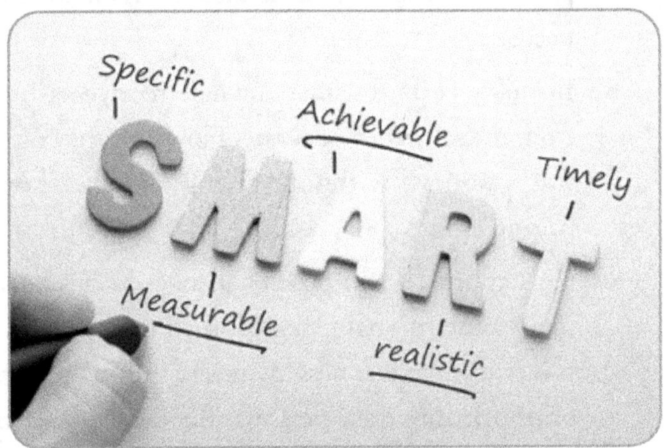

- Breaking down goals into smaller milestones makes them more attainable and manageable.

- Suppliers, vendor payment, business expenses should be made in accordance with the agreed payment terms. This will enhance the credibility and trust of business.

- By honoring payment agreements, businesses can strengthen their reputation and maintain the trust of their suppliers, contributing to long-term success and mutually beneficial partnerships.

Budget your time and money

- The primary goal for a business owner should be to prioritize extracting profits to secure their own financial well-being.

- Unfortunately, many business owners tend to prioritize paying themselves last, neglecting their own financial needs.

- In many cases, business owners receive cash or funds from the sales they generate. However, they often spend this money without giving much thought to prioritization.

- This approach can pose challenges as business owners may unintentionally neglect their own financial needs. It is crucial for business owners to realize the importance of prioritizing their personal finances and setting aside profits for themselves. By doing so, they can ensure their own financial stability and pursue your individual financial goals.

- List all your business expenditure categories and create a monthly budget for each of them. Regularly review these budgets on a monthly basis.

- The main objective of a business is to achieve monthly growth in net profit. However, many business owners are unaware of their monthly net profit and solely focus on the turnover of business. It is essential to review the previous month's net profit during the first week of every month to gain insights into the financial performance of the business and make informed decisions accordingly.

Chapter 4

Your Money, Your Freedom

Building a Solid Financial Foundation

The money you earn as profit belongs to you, while other receipts are allocated to various stakeholders such as suppliers, staff, taxes Etc.

Every month, the business owner should withdraw his net profit.

Net profit = Revenue/Sales + Income from other sources– Cost of Goods Sold – Operating Expenses – Other Expenses– Interest – Depreciation – Taxes.

For example, if you generate sales of 30 Lacs in a month and your net profit is 15%, your actual net profit would amount to 4.5 lacs. This is your actual money, However, In many cases, a businessman assumes that the entire all 30 lac is their money and may be influenced by others to utilize it. This approach can lead to cash crunch over time.

In reality, business owners must plan their net profit in an efficient way to secure future needs.

Let's understand how to plan using an important strategy that is proven to be perfect for every business. I call this "Keep Money Well Strategy."

In above example, 4.5 Lacs net profit should be withdrawn from your business and allocate to different bank accounts.

Open 6 Bank accounts in bank, Label these accounts in your understanding as

- Daily Monthly Expense A/c
- Investment A/c
- Travel A/c
- Self Education A/c
- Savings A/c
- Donation A/c

In the first week of every month, allocate this amount to six different savings accounts, each serving a specific purpose.

Having six accounts sounds like a lot, but I promise you there's a reason for each one.

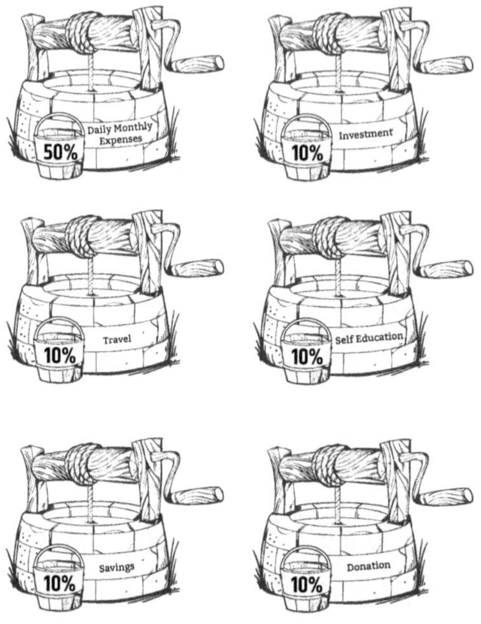

Daily Monthly Expense A/c

- Allocate 50% of your profit to this account for meeting daily and monthly expenses according to your budget.

Investment A/c

- Allocate 10% of your profit to this account for investment purposes, as it is necessary to grow your money.

Travel A/c

- Allocate 10% of your profit to this account for travel & leisure expenses, as they are equally important for spending time with family and friends and rejuvenating yourself.

Self Education A/c

- Allocate 10% of your profit to this account for self-learning and continuous education, as learning should never stop.

Savings A/c

- Allocate 10% of your profit to this account for savings, as it is Important for handling any unforeseen emergencies.

Donation A/c

- Allocate 10% of your profit to this account for making donations, as it is your turn to give back to the society. Remember, the more you give, the more you will receive.

- Trust me, I am sharing based on my personal experience, and the above roadmap serves as a guide to roadmap for becoming financially affluent.

- Start with any amount to build a practice and habit, and make sure to do it during the first week of every month.

Chapter 5

Achieving Financial Success

A Business should maintain a cash reserve for a minimum 3-4 months, and ideally up to 9-12 months.

A cash reserve is set aside to cover expenses in case there is no income from the business. Expenses can be met from that cash reserve. This cash serves as a safety net, ensuring that essential expenses can be met without relying solely on incoming revenue.

- Fixed Assets or Capital Expenditure should be purchased only 20% of the net profit of business.

- Example - If your net profit in a year is 50 Lacs, and the business owner intends to purchase a car, the amount allocated for the car should not exceed 10 Lacs (20% of Rs 50 Lacs).

- By adhering to this approach, the business ensures that a substantial portion of its profits is preserved for other crucial needs, such as reinvestment, expansion, or handling unforeseen expenses.

- Cash credit facilities or loans should be avoided as much as possible.

- The problem with CC Limit is that it does not reach zero, which means you will always have debt.

- If you already have a CC limit, the first action to take should be to clear it before building a cash reserve.

- If you have to take loan, it should be a term loan or a drop line overdraft (OD) that reduces to zero within a certain period of time

- Your working capital loan should not exceed 20% of your turnover.

Manage risks instead of avoiding them

Insurance is a vital part of risk management and financial planning, as it provides protection and financial security.

Stock and building insurance are essential for safeguarding your business assets.

The most important part of stock insurance is ensuring full coverage.

- Example: If the highest inventory value reaches 1 crore on a specific date in a year, the stock Insurance should be obtained for 1 crore.

- Building insurance should always be obtained with a restatement clause.

- Example: Let's say you constructed a building 5 years ago for 75 Lacs, and if that building gets demolished now, the new construction cost today is 1.25 crores. By having insurance with a restatement clause, you would receive the value based on today's cost.

Same way, Life Insurance and Health insurance are equally important for the well-being of your family.

- They provide financial independence and protection from any contingency
- It ensures that your family does not suffer in case of any adverse conditions.

Conclusion: Your Path to Financial Abundance

In conclusion, throughout this book, we have explored various strategies and insights aimed at helping you achieve financial success. Let's recap the key learnings and strategies discussed:

- Understanding the importance of financial literacy and the need to know your numbers. By gaining a solid understanding of financial statements, key performance indicators, and cash flow management, you will be equipped to make informed decisions and effectively manage your business finances.

- Budgeting and planning for profit are essential elements of business success. Creating a realistic budget, forecasting future financials, and controlling costs are crucial steps in effectively managing your resources and maximizing profitability.

- Embracing technology and utilizing financial management tools can streamline operations, improve efficiency, and provide valuable insights to drive financial success.

- Planning for the future encompasses various aspects such as expansion and diversification, financing and investment strategies, and exit planning. By evaluating growth opportunities, securing capital for expansion, and formulating exit strategies, businesses can ensure long-term financial growth, stability, and wealth preservation.

- Throughout this book, my goal has been to inspire and motivate you to take action. Financial success is within your reach, but it requires commitment, discipline, and strategic decision-making. By implementing the strategies and insights shared in this book, you can empower yourself to achieve financial success, both personally and as a business owner.

- Remember, the journey to financial success is unique for each individual, and it may necessitate making adjustments along the way. Stay adaptable, continue learning, and celebrate milestones and achievements as you progress on your path to financial success.

- Now is the moment to seize control of your financial future and shape the life you aspire to. With dedication and perseverance, you have the power to achieve your goals and create lasting financial success. Empower yourself, take decisive action, and wholeheartedly embrace the boundless opportunities that await you. Your financial success awaits you!

Next Step

Are you a business owner in the Indian women's wear industry? Do you want to achieve financial self-sufficiency and expand your business with ease? Look no further! With my extensive 15 years of experience, I have successfully assisted numerous business owners in attaining a lucrative cash flow and generating substantial wealth for themselves.

Join me on this journey to financial success and let's make your business thrive.

- Reach out to me today at vb@mnfashions.com and let's discuss how I can assist you in achieving financial independence while crafting women's wear that is alluring, resilient, and affordable, ensuring that every woman radiates beauty.

- Don't allow the day-to-day operations of your business hold you back from important aspects like personal and business finance. Together, we can ensure that you possess the financial security to support your family's requirements and concentrate on expanding your business. Take the first step towards financial freedom and reach out to me at vb@mnfashions.com.

- Invest in your business and your future today. Contact me now, and let's embark on this journey towards financial success, fostering the flourishing of the Indian women's wear industry.

*"Don't work for money;
make it work for you."*

~Robert Kiyosaki

NOTES:

NOTES:

NOTES:

NOTES: